Rosa Parks
Meet a Civil Rights Hero

Edith Hope Fine

Enslow Publishers, Inc.
40 Industrial Road   PO Box 38
Box 398   Aldershot
Berkeley Heights, NJ 07922 Hants GU12 6BP
USA   UK
http://www.enslow.com

Library of Congress Cataloging-in-Publication Data

Fine, Edith Hope.
   Rosa Parks : meet a civil rights hero / Edith Hope Fine.
     p. cm. — (Meeting famous people)
  Includes index.
  Summary: A biography of a woman whose actions led to the desegregation of buses in Montgomery, Alabama, in the 1960s and who was an important figure in the early days of the civil rights movement.
  ISBN 0-7660-2099-1 (hardcover)
  1. Parks, Rosa, 1913– . Juvenile literature. 2. African Americans—Alabama—Montgomery—Biography—Juvenile literature. 3. African American civil rights workers—Alabama—Montgomery—Biography—Juvenile literature. 4. Civil rights workers—Alabama—Montgomery—Biography—Juvenile literature. 5. Segregation in transportation—Alabama—Montgomery—History—20th century—Juvenile literature. 6. Montgomery (Ala.)—Biography—Juvenile literature. 7. Montgomery (Ala.)—Race relations—Juvenile literature. 1. Parks, Rosa, 1913– . 2. Civil rights workers. 3. African Americans—Biography. 4. Women—Biography.] I. Title. II. Series.
  F334.M753 P3839 2003
  323'.092—dc21

                                         2002010406

Illustration Credits: AP/Wide World Photos, pp. 3, 16, 23, 28; Enslow Publishers, Inc., pp. 19, 29; From the Collections of Henry Ford Museum & Greenfield Village, pp. 1, 2, 21; Library of Congress, pp. 6, 7, 8, 9, 11, 12, 13, 17, 18, 25; Photographs and Prints Division, Schomburg Center for Research in Black Culture, The New York Public Library, Astor, Lenox and Tilden Foundations, pp. 4, 26, 27; Smithsonian Institution, p. 14.

Cover Illustrations: Photographs and Prints Division, Schomburg Center for Research in Black Culture, The New York Public Library, Astor, Lenox and Tilden Foundations. Streetcar interior: Smithsonian Institution.

Table of Contents

Rosa Parks is often called
the mother of the civil rights movement.

Chapter 1

Growing Up in Alabama

When Rosa Parks was a child in the South, black people had to sit at the back of the bus. They could not eat at restaurants with white people. White children and black children could not go to the same schools or walk side by side. They could not sit together at the movies or at ball games.

Rosa never dreamed that one day she would help change all that.

Blacks and whites could not use the same water fountains.

Rosa Louise McCauley was born on February 4, 1913, in Tuskegee, Alabama. Her mother, Leona, taught school. Her father, James, was a carpenter who built houses. He left the family when Rosa was two.

Rosa and her younger brother, Sylvester, lived on a farm with their mother and their grandparents. The farm was in Pine Level, near Montgomery, Alabama. Poor but loving, Rosa's grandparents were hard workers. They grew much of their own food.

Both of them had been slaves in Alabama. Back then, they had lived on a big farm called a plantation. They worked in the fields, planting and picking cotton. Rosa's grandfather told of having no shoes, feeling hungry, and being beaten. Rosa listened. She knew that no one should be treated that way.

Rosa was a quiet girl. She was happy weaving baskets of corn husks or catching crayfish. She felt at home in church, with its joyful music. For her, learning Bible lessons was easy.

Rosa could read by the time she was four. At age six, Rosa started school. She loved books, counting, and outdoor games.

In the South, all the schools for white children were better than the schools for black children. White

Picking cotton in the hot sun was hard, miserable work.

children rode buses to brick schools with glass windows. They had new books and supplies. White schools were open nine months a year.

Black children had no buses. Rosa and her brother walked eight miles to school. Their few books were old. More than fifty children were crowded into one room. The windows had wood shutters, no glass,

White children's schools had plenty of books and supplies.

and icy cold winds chilled the air. Black children had to plant and pick cotton on the farms, so their school year was only five months long.

To Rosa, all these differences were not right.

Schools for black children were crowded and cold.

Chapter 2

Learning About Fairness

Black children like Rosa picked cotton all day long. The hot dirt burned their feet. The work hurt their backs and made their fingers bleed. Often, white farmers beat their workers.

Rosa knew that some white people were kind. She liked going fishing with her white neighbor. But it was very hard being African American in the South. Laws kept blacks and whites apart. This is called segregation.

The Ku Klux Klan (KKK), a white hate group, beat and killed African Americans for no reason. Rosa sometimes sat up at night with her grandfather. He kept a loaded shotgun by the door in case the KKK ever came.

When Rosa was eleven, her mother sent her to a private school in Montgomery, Alabama. She lived with Aunt Fannie, her mother's sister. A few years later, when she was in eleventh grade at Booker T. Washington High

Members of the Ku Klux Klan spread terror through the South and taught hatred to their children.

School, Rosa had to leave school. Her grandmother and her mother were sick. They needed her help.

In 1931, Rosa met Raymond Parks, a barber. Raymond shared Rosa's belief that all people should be treated fairly. They married in December 1932. She was nineteen years old.

Few African Americans finished high school in those days, but Rosa knew she could do it. In 1933, Rosa, age twenty, graduated from high school.

All over America, times were hard in the 1930s. Jobs were few. Jobs for black people were even fewer. To earn money, Rosa did some sewing and worked in an office.

Raymond Parks often helped African Americans in trouble with the police. Rosa knew this was dangerous. Still, he kept on. From her family, teachers, and husband, Rosa learned to believe in herself and to stand up for what was right.

People once had to obey signs like these.

In the South, Rosa and other African Americans
had to sit at the back of buses and streetcars.

Chapter 3

Working for Change

In 1941, Rosa Parks had a job at Maxwell Field, an army base near Montgomery, Alabama. Riding the buses to work, Rosa saw an important difference.

Montgomery city buses had two doors. Blacks had to enter through the front door to pay their fare. Then they had to get off the bus and get back on through the rear door. Sometimes, even after they paid their money, the bus drove away without them.

On the city buses, Rosa had to sit at the back. But on the army bus, she could sit anywhere. Rosa liked that freedom.

In 1943, Rosa joined the National Association for the Advancement of Colored People (NAACP). This group was working for freedom—for all people to be treated fairly. Rosa became secretary of the NAACP in Montgomery. She kept records of cruel treatment of black people. She made phone calls and wrote letters for the NAACP.

Rosa saw that African Americans were treated badly. That made her sad—and angry, too.

16

One big NAACP goal was to get African Americans to vote in elections. For white people, signing up to vote was easy. But for black people, there were problems.

A registration office might be open only when most blacks were at work. Or the office might suddenly close just as a black person's turn came. Blacks had to take reading tests and pay voting fees. Whites did not.

Members of the NAACP worked for freedom and fairness.

When Rosa tried to register in 1943, her voting card never came in the mail. Later that year, she decided to try again. To get there, she had to take a bus. Rosa climbed on and paid her dime. The back doorway was jammed with riders, so she stayed on the bus. The bus driver, James Blake, ordered Rosa to step off the bus and use the other door. She refused.

DO YOU WANT TO VOTE?
REGISTER HERE
THIS DATE APRIL 1, 1948 FROM 10:30 AM - 5:00 P.M.
CO-SPONSORED BY ALPHA PHI ALPHA FRAT. & NAACP YM CO.

It was often hard for African Americans
to register to vote.

James Blake was a racist. He believed white people were better than blacks. He called black people nasty names. Sometimes he would spit tobacco at them from his bus window.

Blake pulled Rosa's sleeve. She warned him not to touch her. In her quiet way, Rosa showed her anger. She dropped her purse, and, to pick it up, she sat down in a seat for white people. Then she stepped off the bus. She did not register to vote that day.

After that, every time Rosa Parks saw James Blake driving a bus, she walked or waited for a different bus.

In 1944, Rosa tried again to register to vote. She was a good reader, yet she was told she had failed the reading test. Rosa knew that could not be true. The next year, she tried again and passed.

At last, Rosa Parks could vote.

Chapter 4

Rosa Parks Stays Seated

Working as NAACP secretary, Rosa typed hundreds of reports. They told of African Americans who were beaten, shot, or killed by racist white Americans full of hatred. Rosa also knew that during World War II, her brother and other black soldiers fought bravely for the United States. But when they came back from the war in Europe, they were treated badly.

All these wrongs, Rosa Parks remembered.

Rosa thought, too, about the buses that she and other African Americans rode to work. Ten seats in front were for whites only. Ten seats in back could be used by blacks. The bus drivers were in charge of the middle seats. They placed a sign to show where blacks had to sit. All African Americans had to stay behind the sign.

The NAACP wanted to end this bus segregation.

By now, Rosa, age forty-two, was living with her husband and mother in a tiny apartment. She worked at a department store as a seamstress—pinning, pressing, and sewing clothes.

On Thursday, December 1, 1955, the chilly Montgomery streets were decorated for Christmas. After a long workday, Rosa boarded a bus for home.

Rosa took a seat in the middle of the bus. There were still four seats open for whites. When five white people got on the bus, one man was left standing.

The bus driver ordered the black riders to move back. No one did.

Again he asked. This time he was angry.

The other three blacks moved, but Rosa Parks stayed seated. She saw then that the driver was James Blake. He asked Rosa if she was going to move.

"No," she said.

Blake told her he would call the police, and they would put her in jail.

"You may do that," she said.

The police came. At the police station, officers took Rosa's picture and fingerprinted her. Then they locked her in a jail cell.

She asked for water but was not given any.

A police officer took Rosa's fingerprints.

She asked three times before she was allowed to call home. Rosa's mother and husband were very upset. They called some white friends and asked for help getting Rosa out of jail.

Chapter 5

Rosa Helps Civil Rights

Word spread fast that Rosa Parks had been in jail. Some important African Americans in Montgomery called a meeting. They chose Martin Luther King, Jr., to be their leader. They asked Rosa to help them fight in court for fair laws for blacks. As a protest, they planned to boycott all the buses in Montgomery. They wanted African Americans to stop riding city buses. Then the bus companies would lose money. Could this help change the law?

Thousands of flyers were printed for black schools, churches, and families. "Stay off the buses on Monday," they read. "Don't ride the bus to work, to town, to school, or any place. . . . Take a cab or share a ride, or walk."

Martin Luther King, Jr., led the protest against the city buses.

That Sunday, Martin Luther King, Jr., and other preachers talked about Rosa Parks. She was calm, polite, and hardworking, they said. She knew right from wrong. And segregation was wrong. Dr. King told African Americans that it was time "to gain justice on the buses in this city."

An amazing thing happened the next day. The date

was Monday, December 5. All over the city, African Americans took taxis, drove in carpools, or walked. They did not ride the buses.

And the boycott lasted. Month after month, in good weather and bad, African Americans stayed off the buses. Montgomery city buses were almost empty for more than a year. On December 20, 1956, judges in the Supreme Court—the highest court in the United States—spoke. Alabama's segregation laws were unfair, they said. All people had to be treated the same.

Rosa spoke out for equal rights for all people.

African Americans cheered.

The bravery of Rosa Parks helped to start the civil rights movement. Across the country, people of all races worked together to make laws equal for everyone.

Rosa Parks did her part. She spoke at meetings, schools, and churches. Everywhere she went, people came to hear her talk about freedom and fairness.

In 1957, Rosa moved with her husband and mother to Detroit, Michigan. In 1965, she took a job as an assistant to Congressman John Conyers. She worked for him for the next twenty-three years.

Over the years, Rosa has won many awards.

Later years were hard on Rosa Parks. Martin Luther King, Jr., the civil rights leader, was killed in 1968. Rosa's husband and her brother both died in 1977, and her mother died in 1979.

Good things happened, too. Rosa received thousands of letters thanking her for what she did. Streets, schools, and libraries all over the country were named for her. In 1987, she started the Rosa and Raymond Parks Institute for Self-Development to help more young people get an education and to teach them about civil rights.

"As long as a child needs help, as long as people are not free, there will be work to do," said Rosa.

Rosa Parks said "no" on a bus in Montgomery, Alabama, in 1955.

Today, people around the world honor her as a hero—an ordinary person who helped change history.

Timeline

1913~Born February 4 in Tuskegee, Alabama.

1924~Starts school in Montgomery, Alabama.

1932~Marries Raymond Parks.

1933~Earns her high school diploma.

1943~Becomes secretary of the Montgomery branch of the National Association for the Advancement of Colored People (NAACP).

1945~Becomes a registered voter after four tries.

1955~Arrested on December 1 for refusing to obey segregation laws.

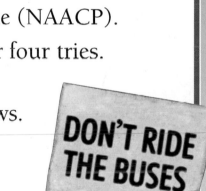

DON'T RIDE THE BUSES

1965–1988~Works as an assistant to Congressman John Conyers.

1987~Cofounds the Rosa and Raymond Parks Institute for Self-Development.

1996~Receives the Presidential Medal of Freedom.

1999~Receives the Congressional Gold Medal.

boycott—To refuse to buy a product or a service as a way to protest something that is unfair.

civil rights movement—People working together to give all citizens equal rights under the law.

colored—A word once used for African Americans.

National Association for the Advancement of Colored People (NAACP)—A group started to help all Americans gain equal rights and protection under the law.

Presidential Medal of Freedom—The highest honor given by the United States government.

segregation—The policy of keeping whites and blacks apart.

slave—A person who is owned by another person and forced to work for no pay.

Learn More

Books

Adler, David A. *A Picture Book of Rosa Parks.*
New York: Holiday House, 1997.

Greenfield, Eloise. *Rosa Parks.*
New York: HarperCollins Publishers, 1999.

Parks, Rosa, and James Haskins. *I Am Rosa Parks:
My Bus Ride to Freedom.* New York: Penguin
Putnam Books for Young Readers, 1997.

Internet Addresses

A short biography plus lots of links.
<http://www.africanamericans.com/RosaParks.htm/>

Information from the Troy State University
Montgomery Rosa Parks Library and Museum in
Montgomery, Alabama
<http://www.tsum.edu/museum/parksbio.htm>

Index